BOOK OF SOLACE

Sometimes all you have to do
is open your heart and listen.

Book of Solace

Love and Light for Dark Days

Anja Steensig

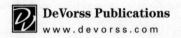

DeVorss Publications
www.devorss.com

Book of Solace
Copyright © 2022
by Anja Steensig

ISBN Print Edition: 978-087516-926-2
ISBN Ebook Edition: 978-087516-925-5

Library of Congress Control Number: 2022035173
First DeVorss Publications Edition, 2023

Printed in The United States of America

DeVorss & Company, Publishers
PO Box 1389
Camarillo CA 93011-1389
www.devorss.com

———

The original Danish edition
"En lille bog til mørke dage - Trøst i tro og kærlighed"
Published in Denmark by SUPERLUX, 2020
English translation by Nina Sokol

Library of Congress Cataloging-in-Publication Data
Names: Steensig, Anja, 1973- author.
Title: Book of solace : love and light for dark days / Anja Steensig.
Description: Camarillo : DeVorss Publications, [2023] | Summary:
    "Anja Steensig of Denmark rebuilds her life from the sole perspective of Love. No religion is needed, no guru, no church. The source is within each person, always ready to be received."-- Provided by publisher.
Identifiers: LCCN 2022035173 | ISBN 9780875169262 (paperback) | ISBN 9780875169255 (ebook)
Subjects: LCSH: Love. | Self-actualization (Psychology)
Classification: LCC BF575.L8 S757 2023 | DDC 152.4/1--dc23/eng/20220930
LC record available at https://lccn.loc.gov/2022035173

TABLE OF CONTENTS

Dedicated in gratitude
To those without whom
My life would be poorer,
My world would be smaller,
My sky would seem darker.
Your presence is my light.

THERE IS A LOVE SO POWERFUL
THAT IT CAN HEAL ANY WOUND.
UNCONDITIONAL AND ETERNAL,
INFINITE AND ALL-ENCOMPASSING.
IT IS YOURS TO RECEIVE.

WILL YOU SAY YES?

My beloved friend,

Thank you for picking up this book in your time of need.

It is a true honor for me to take your hand and accompany you into the solace of unconditional Love.

I am here to remind you that you are never alone.

Even on the darkest of days when the pain of feeling lost and abandoned drags you into a state of hopelessness, and it feels like no one will ever be able to really understand the suffering you are going through, you are not alone.

In every step, you are held. In every breath, you are loved.

I am here to remind you that even the hours of despair hold a spark of light. A seed settling into the dust from where it will begin its transformational journey into life and beauty.

I am here to remind you that within your heart is a place of sanctuary. A sacred place where you can find shelter. Where you are unbreakable. The realm of unconditional Love.

Right now life might seem difficult or even terrifying. It may seem like you are completely on your own and in the dark, struggling and stumbling without direction. But let me share something with you:

It was not until I was broken and stripped of every possible defense, that I found the courage to be vulnerable enough to truly open the gates of my heart.

Beyond these gates, I found the kingdom of Love. The kingdom of my soul. The kingdom of God. An infinite ocean of unconditional Love, so powerful that I could only surrender.

So I succumbed to the truth of my soul and my life was changed forever.

I realized that through Love I was stronger than I imagined. Through Love, I saw clearer than ever. Through Love, I began to recognize Love in everything. Through Love, I was lovable. Through Love, there was nothing or no one unlovable. Through Love, I fell in love with the world. In Love, I was never alone.

I pray that you may enter these sacred gates of your heart to experience the presence of this Love. It is your innate treasure.

No religion is needed, no guru, no church. There is nothing you have to do, to be or to believe, to deserve this Love. It is always there and it is always yours to receive.

This is why I am writing to you today. As I step aside to allow the voice of Love to speak through me, I will provide a space where you can rest for a while. A space of solace and hope dedicated to reminding you of the eternal light you carry within.

Read it in any order that you feel inspired to. Dwell in the presence of every text. Contemplate. Meditate on them and allow

the words to reach you through the heart,
as this book was never written for the mind.
This is just solace. The solace of Love itself.
Receive.

Bless you.
With Love, Anja

Surrender into Love

I KNOW YOU FEEL BROKEN, MY LOVE,
BUT YOU ARE UNBREAKABLE.

I KNOW YOU FEEL LOST, MY LOVE,
BUT YOU ARE RIGHT THERE.

I KNOW YOU FEEL ALONE, MY LOVE,
BUT I AM RIGHT HERE.

LET ME bring you solace
on this day of your despair.
LET ME clear the way
for you to come up after air.

LET ME wipe the tears of pain
and sorrow off your face.
LET ME hold you firmly
in the arms of LOVE'S embrace.

LET ME draw you close into
the realm of LOVE and light.
LET the veil uncover
what you carry deep inside.

A Prayer

Hold me, my beloved,
Let me rest here for a while.
Hold me, my beloved,
I can't force another smile.

Hold me, my beloved,
Sit beside me as I weep.
Hold me, my beloved,
Keep me safe here while I sleep.

Hold me, my beloved,
I surrender in Your arm.
Hold me, my beloved,
reinstate my peace and calm.

Hold me, my beloved,
As the darkness passes through.
Hold me, my beloved,
till I find the light in You.

LEAN INTO ME, MY PRECIOUS HEART,
LET ALL YOUR WORRIES GO.
LEAN INTO ME, MY LOVE, MY LIFE,
LET ALL YOUR FACES SHOW.

IN EVERY BREATH, I WILL BE THERE
TO HOLD YOU THROUGH THE PAIN.
WITH EVERY BREATH YOU TAKE,
I'LL WHISPER WORDS TO KEEP YOU SANE.

SURRENDER, MY BELOVED CHILD,
I'LL CARRY YOU TONIGHT.
SURRENDER AS I SHOW YOU
TO THE PORTAL OF YOUR MIGHT.

Lost in the darkness
of shadows and gloom,
Drowning in heartbreaking pains
of my doom,
Trying to scream out
but choke from the fear,
Alone in an abyss
where no one comes near.

Desperately calling Your name
in despair,
Kicking and struggling
to come up for air,
Reaching my arms
toward heaven in plea,
Please God, oh please,
come and set my soul free.

As I surrendered,
exhausted from fight,
Into my darkness
came glimpses of light.

Gently they grew
as my fear seemed to ease,
Soothing my body
and mind like a breeze.

Held in the arms
of Your true Love's embrace,
Finally knowing
the truth of Your grace,
I could rise up
from the ashes of old,
Finding inside me
Your treasure of gold.

Beloved soul, hand over your pain.
Release your shame, your guilt, your fear.
Let go of all your worry, troubles, and grief.
Allow God to hold in Love
everything you find unlovable,
everything you find wrong, ugly, unworthy,
stupid, less than and undeserving,
everything that ever made you feel not
good enough,
everything difficult,
everything scary,
everything dark.
There is nothing Love cannot hold.

A Prayer

Dear God,
I will lie down
for a while.
Please hold me
while I rest.

Dear God,
I will give up
for a while.
Please watch me
while I nest.

Dear God,
I surrender
all my struggles,
all my fight.

Dear God,
Please, just see me through
the darkness of this night.

My loved one, let Me in.

As I knock on the door to your heart,

I'm asking you to allow Me to love you

unconditionally.

I worship everything you are:

Your strength,

Your weakness,

Your shame and your pride,

Your light and your darkness,

Your joy and your sadness,

Your fear and your power.

It is all perfect to me.

Listen to my whisper

as I call your name from the kingdom

in your heart.

FEARLESSLY LET IT OPEN—

THE DOOR TO YOUR SOUL—

FOR YOU TO FEEL MY LOVE,

FOR YOU TO HEAR MY GUIDANCE,

FOR YOU TO SURRENDER IN MY ARMS,

THE ARMS OF YOUR OWN SOUL,

YOUR DIVINITY,

LOVE ITSELF,

GOD.

WE ARE ONE, MY LOVE.

INSEPARABLE.

IN LOVE.

On cold days like this
my longing grows stronger.
I can't feel You in the dark.

Reaching, calling, moving
here and there to catch
a glimpse of Your sacred light.
Forgetting in my pain
that all I need to do
is lean back,
surrender and say yes.
Yes my love: I am Yours.

And light returns.

There is a place you can rest,
in the arms of the all-loving
mother-father.
Breathe there.
Surrender in the embrace,
peaceful as a baby.

Beloved soul, I wish you knew how treasured you are. How absolutely loved you are.

I know there are things in your life that hurt you. There are people, experiences and situations that make you happy, make you smile and make you feel lighthearted. There are thoughts that make you feel insecure, events that make you lose your balance and experiences that make you feel insufficient. I don't know this because I know you personally. I know it because you are a human being. We are very good at hiding it, but you should know that all people struggle.

Behind the facades of appearance, personality, character traits, upbringing, culture, style, career and all the other things we base our and others' identities on, we are the same. All we really want is to love and be loved, and all pain derives from that longing.

I wish you could see what I see. Namely, that Love lives within you. Eternally present and always within reach. Ready to embrace

you so that you can embrace life and yourself in it—completely as it is. Meanwhile I
will treasure you and all the fine things that
you are. And hope that you someday will
discover and acknowledge your own innate
treasure of unconditional Love.

You are something very special.

There is no one exactly like you. No one
else who can be you and contribute to the
world with precisely the things that you
bring. There is a reason why you are the
way you are, namely, to be you. The world
needs your unique contribution and if you
try to be someone or something else you are
denying the world of what you are here to
give it. Know that there is someone waiting
for you to be that.

You have an infinite amount of goodness
within you.

Within your core runs a source of the
purest Love. A Love that is eternal and
impossible to run out of. A Love that will

uplift and nourish the people that you meet. A Love that will uplift and nourish yourself. A Love that can embrace any fear so that you can breathe freely and find the courage to be everything you are. Your love can change the world, and there is a need for you. You matter more than you think.

You are stronger than you think.

Once you have found the key to the source of your Love, you will find that even though the world offers you resistance, even though life can be so heavy to bear that it is hard to breathe, the path to the light above the surface has become so much shorter. You will find that a single breath can call in the embrace of Love itself. That Love is only a dedicated thought away.

You will find that your true strength is not found in external circumstances that can be taken away from you. Money, beauty, power and health can all be taken away from you in a split second. Your true strength is the

Love that fully embraces you precisely as you are, that holds you with such care and allows you to feel exactly what you are feeling, that fills you and makes you stand tall, that doesn't allow you to let others take advantage of you and walk all over you, that motivates you to be kind to others and, not least, be kind to yourself first. The Love that you are here to give to this world gives you the strength to rise to the challenge.

Thy will be done.
Not my will,
but Yours.

Thy will be done.
Not my will,
but Yours.

Thy will be done.
Not my will,
but Yours.

Thy will be done.
Not my will,
but Yours.

Thy will be done.
Not my will,
but Yours.

Treasure Your Emotions

Beloved soul, you are
allowed to be sad,
allowed to grieve,
allowed to be angry,
allowed to be worried,
allowed to feel insecure and small,
allowed to feel life as a heavy burden on
your exhausted shoulders.

Every emotion is your birthright.
And when you sit with them, listen to them,
hold them, they will show you that all they
ever needed was your loving attention.

Let the sorrow cut you deeper.
Let the pain and loss sink in.
Just allow yourself to feel
the kiss of life upon your skin.

Please don't fight it.
Please don't fix it.
Please let tears stream down your face.

Please just hold yourself
with all there is
in true Love's firm embrace.

THE FEAR, MY LOVE, IS CALLING YOU
TO WAKE UP FROM YOUR SLEEP.
THE FEAR, MY LOVE, IS PENETRATING
ARMORS AS YOU WEEP.

THE FEAR, MY LOVE, IS BREAKING DOWN
DEFENSES WITH YOUR TEARS.
THE LOVE, MY LOVE, IS WAKING
FROM THE CRY OUT OF YOUR FEARS.

THE PAIN, MY LOVE, IS SHAKING YOU
AND BRINGING YOU BACK HOME.
THE PAIN, MY LOVE, IS SHEDDING LIGHT
ON DARK STREETS WHERE YOU ROAM.

YOUR PAIN, MY LOVE, WILL PEEL OFF
UNTRUE LAYERS YOU RETAIN.
YOUR LOVE, MY LOVE, WILL COME ALIVE
WHEN CALLED OUT BY YOUR PAIN.

Beloved soul, have you noticed how those feelings of yours can toss you about, with such overpowering force that they take up all the space, blind you and swallow you up until you are no longer able to tell what's what and you equate them with yourself? Feelings such as *I am angry, I am afraid, I am happy, I am sad*.

But what is a feeling really other than a fleeting physical sensation, a message from your body telling you that something is at play within you? It is not until you start the mental storytelling machine, that it becomes more than that.

Applying the usual labels that are so familiar: This is happiness, this is anger, this is sorrow, this is fear. Judging them: This is a positive feeling, this is a negative feeling, this one is of low frequency, this one is of high frequency, this feeling is unconstructive, ridiculous, useless, wonderful, unwelcome, welcome....

And then spending hours pondering their source. Who, what, why? Each and every feeling has an entire life story attached to it. Explaining it. "I always get sad when... because it reminds me of the time when... and I'm just that sort of person who...."

I ask you to let go of them. The labels, the judgments and the sources.

The physical messages we call feelings are nothing but pieces of information to you about where to bring your attention. Your love.

So when they come rushing forth in their calling for loving attention, that is precisely what you should give them. For when we choose the opposite, when we choose to ignore them, to fight against them, to subdue them, then they will just call out for your attention more and more loudly.

Your feelings are an equal part of you, and when you deny them you are also denying a part of yourself. It is an ongoing internal war that will only stop on the very day that you allow yourself to feel the precise emotions that you feel.

No feeling is wrong. No feeling is shameful. No feeling is forbidden. Feelings are here only to help you navigate your love in the right direction.

Treasure your emotions, my beloved, as they awaken you from the slumber of forgetting.

The fear, the despair, the sorrow, the pain, the anger, the jealousy, the shame, the worthlessness are all like little children, crying from a bad dream, reaching up their arms in longing for the affection and comfort of their mother. Waking her out of her dream state into remembrance of the reality of who she is. Your emotions are calling you to wake up and ignite your unconditionally loving soul. The all-encompassing mother of your higher being.

So please, my love, take one step back and close your eyes. Imagine that your breathing goes in and out through your heart. Allow your heart to become softer and warmer as you breathe. Perhaps thinking of a person, an animal or a spiritual figure that awakens feelings of love within you. Sense whether you are able to call forth a feeling of love and gratitude.

If there is even the smallest spark of love, you can use your breathing to make it grow. Imagine that you are inhaling pure love and filling your heart more and more with each breath you take. Allow yourself to linger in this state of love until you feel you have a good grasp of it.

Then let go of it and call forth instead the difficult feeling that is weighing on your mind today, not the cause of it, not the story behind why you feel that way right now, just the feeling itself.

Give it as much space as you dare to for you to really feel it. Now start exploring inside your body. Notice where the feeling that is taking up so much space at the moment is manifested. Where is it located? Curiously dive into an exploration of the way it expresses itself in your body.

How does it really feel? Is it heavy, sharp, trembling? Does it have a shape? A color? Allow yourself to examine it without judging it or labeling it. Meet it with an open curiosity and with all of your senses. Look closely at the child that is your emotion and as you watch it, notice that the emotion is separate from you. And now recall the love and gratitude you called forth in your heart before, and let it flow to the spot where the difficult emotion is located. Give it the loving attention it is calling for, without feeding it the stories of why it came or what gave it life in the first place. It is not here to remind you of the source of its existence. It is here for your attention and for your Love, here to let you know that you are desperately needed.

Be its mother.

Be its father.

Pick it up in your arms.

Hold it.

Caress it.

No emotion is too ugly, too shameful, too difficult to receive true Love.

Acknowledge it.

Give it your attention.

Hold space for it to act out, while you calmly watch in compassion.

Whisper in its ear:

"My precious child, I've got you.

I love you.

I am here for you—always."

Hold it as an infant close to your heart. Allow the feeling of tenderness and compassion to flow into it, and see how it, with a sigh of satisfied relief, falls back to sleep. Tender as a baby. Ready to wake up screaming the moment it yet again needs the soothing embrace of its mother. And you will be there. Ready to hold and to love again.

This is what you are capable of.

Every difficult emotion has the capacity to wake you up to the realization of the unconditional love of your soul.

Every time the earth trembles under your feet, shaking you to the core, God is showing you the way back into the essence of your soul. Shaking off the armor of who you thought you were supposed to be. Leading you back home to who you came to be. Reminding you of who you are.

And so every life crisis, every goodbye, every darkness holds the potential of a new beginning that will spark a transformation back into your light, into Love.

A Prayer

Precious feeling,
May I find the strength today
to face you and embrace you
with everything you are.

May I have the courage to feel you
in your full expression.

May I allow you into my heart
so you no longer need to knock
on the door.

May I see you today as the
messenger you are, and may I meet you
in your call for my love.

May I give you the attention you
long for, and may I acknowledge
you as being a part of me.

May I find peace and faith
so that we may live side by side.
There is plenty of space for both of us.

Thank you for everything you have
shown and taught me.

I see you.

I love you.

Amen.

Longing

Beloved soul, I know the emptiness you feel, the longing for something you forgot.

The longing to be known, to be loved, to be reconnected with the truth of your soul.

The longing to reconnect with the source of everything, your origin, Love.

Maybe you have searched in churches or mosques, or in books of new age–old age wisdom.

Maybe you found a philosophy, a guru, a temple, a system or a priest that answered your longing and brought you to God. Beautiful. Walk the path that fills you with joy.

But know this: God is right here. Always. And all you have to do to experience the eternal embrace of Love is to say yes.

You need no translator, no mediator, no religion, no permission, no rituals, no rules.

The kingdom of God is within. Yours to access whenever you are ready. God will be there waiting. Rejoicing in your return.

What is this longing
moving my heart,
pulling me,
swaying me,
calling me?

What is this softness
melting my defense,
loving me,
soothing me,
calling me?

What is this fierceness
knowing my truth,
moving me,
showing me,
calling me?

Is it You, my love?
Is it You?

Follow the longing,
my love.
Follow the longing.

Let the pull of your heart
draw you closer
to the source of
your eternal light.

To the Love that will
light up your darkness
and make you feel safe
through the night.

Follow the longing,
my love.
Follow the longing.

A Prayer

My heart is on fire
longing for You,
longing for everything
loving and true.

In books and in churches
I longed to be near,
not knowing Your presence
was already here.

My heart is soon bursting
longing for You,
knowing You're longing
to meet with me too.

Beloved, just pull me in,
show me the way.
From now and forever,
with You I will stay.

OH MY BELOVED, STOP SEARCHING.
IT IS ALL RIGHT HERE.

EVERYTHING YOU LONGED FOR,
EVERYTHING YOUR SOUL
WAS ACHING TO FIND,
YOUR PURPOSE IN LIFE,
THE COURAGE TO WALK YOUR PATH,
THE STRENGTH TO CARRY ON,
AND TRUE LOVE.
ABOVE ALL, HERE IS
MY UNCONDITIONAL LOVE.

MY BELOVED, STOP SEARCHING.
IT IS HERE.

For endless days
and endless nights
I have waited for You
to enter my world.

Oh, had I only known
You were always here.

MEET ME IN THE REALM OF LOVE.

CLOSE YOUR EYES.

BREATHE THROUGH YOUR HEART.

REMEMBER LOVE.

YOU ARE THERE.

HUSH, BE SILENT, MY LOVE.

BE SILENT, MY LOVE

AS I WHISPER.

I LOVE YOU.

I AM HERE.

I LOVE YOU.

I AM HERE.

I LOVE YOU.

I AM HERE.

COME MEET ME

IN THE GARDEN

OF YOUR SILENCE.

A Prayer

Oh my Love, draw me closer.
My longing runs so deep
knowing You, breathing You,
sensing You, loving You.
Oh Love, draw me closer.

Oh my Love, let me smell You
in wild roses and lavender,
in raindrops on hot pavement,
in crispy winter nights.
Oh Love, let me smell You.

Oh my Love, let me feel You
in the sweetness of a touch,
in wind caressing chin and cheeks,
in sunlight kissing longing lips.
Oh Love, let me feel You.

Oh my Love, let me see You
behind the curtains of pain,
in random acts of kindness,
in faces lined with joy.
Oh Love, let me see You

LOVE IS HERE.

NEVER ABSENT.

ALWAYS YOURS.

HUSH.

THE DIVINE WHISPERS

OF YOUR HEART

ARE LEADING YOU THERE.

Remembering

Beloved soul, do you know how powerful you are?

I know it is hard to believe on a day like this, when hiding from the world seems like the perfect solution. When you may feel you have nothing to offer. When you may feel unworthy and worthless. Small and insignificant.

But you are capable of creating miracles, my beloved. Even the miracle of loving yourself. The one person in the world that you are foremost responsible for. The one person that needs your love and compassion more than anyone. The one person who should be able to fully rely on you. The one who must be able to trust you with his or her life.

Maybe you will object: "I will never be able to fully love myself" you will say, and you will be right

It is not your human mind that has the capacity for unconditional love, it is your soul. The pure essence of your divinity. And there is nothing and no one your soul cannot love, as it is of God, and God is Love itself. A Love that is always there. A Love that is always the same. Independent of other people. Independent of what is going on in your outer world. Even when you feel completely abandoned and you can find no sign of Love in your life. Love is never absent. Never fragmented, never less than fully there.

So, read this through and then close your eyes to try it on. You don't have to remember the exact words, just the basic principle:

> Allow yourself to take a mental step back to imagine that you can see yourself from the outside, and look at the human being before you.

Can you connect with a feeling of compassion for this person?

TRY:

See the child you used to be.

Remember the longing in her or him to feel
acknowledged, loved, held.

Recognize the pain she or he is experiencing and let it soften your heart as you allow
this child to ignite your compassion.

Feel how bad you want to keep her or him
safe from harm.

Dive into your deep longing to soothe the
pain of the child.

Stay in that longing for a moment, before
you allow yourself to pick up the child and
hold it in your arms.

Caress it. Gently, caringly, tenderly.

Let your love for this child grow
with every breath.

Let it fill you up, for you to pass it on to this
child as you hold it close to your heart.

Now, take a deep breath, let the child turn back into the grown-up that is you.

Remember the longing in her or him to feel acknowledged, loved, held.

Recognize the pain she or he is experiencing and let it soften your heart as you allow this human being to ignite your compassion.

Feel how bad you want to keep her or him safe from harm.

Dive into your deep longing to soothe his or her pain.

Stay in that longing for a moment, before you allow yourself to lovingly embrace this person that is you.

Hold her. Hold him.

Let your Love grow with every breath.

Let it fill you up for you to pass it on to this human as you hold it close to your heart.

Stay there for as long as you can.

Breathe Love.

Could you find it in your heart to Love this human being?

Maybe you felt it straight away. Maybe just a glimpse, maybe not at all, but know that the day when you are able to hold yourself in pure unconditional Love and stay there no matter what happens, is the day when you can stop hiding. Because on that day, when you know deep in your being that you are lovable with everything you are, when you know that you are absolutely loved by Love itself, it will no longer matter what others may think of you.

So, my loved one, the aim is this: Make yourself available for God's unconditional Love to work through you, and give yourself permission to be the primary beneficiary. Because when you acknowledge the truth, that you are Love, and you let the light from this Love illuminate every dark spot of your being, you will be able to meet not only yourself, but the world and everyone in it from a place of spaciousness, acceptance and compassion.

Through prayer, through surrender, through longing, through following that which moves and softens your heart, through allowing yourself to fall in love with what you meet, you will come to remember the truth of your divine nature.

Then you will discover that you are light. That you need no armor because the light shining in you and through you has the capacity to overcome any darkness.

Then you will discover your real strength and courage. Your titanium core, unbreakable.

Then you will discover that you can raise your head in dignity, with your back straight, recognizing the power of your wounds. Unashamed and dignified, no matter how bruised and frayed you thought you were.

Visit your heart. Find yourself kneeling with head bowed in awe at your grandeur.

On dark days
when heaviness creeps in,
when my eyes are closed to
the beauty around me,
when breathing becomes harder,
I close my eyes and recall
the feeling of being held,
the presence of Love
surrounding me.
And I am lifted into the
remembrance of my strength,
my light, my Love, until I am
finally able to hold any heaviness
in the loving embrace of my soul.

BELOVED, LET ME SHOW YOU
ALL YOUR DIGNITY, YOUR GRACE.
FROM STARDUST, YOU WERE
BROUGHT TO LIFE
TO SERVE THE HUMAN RACE.

BELOVED, LET ME SHOW YOU
JUST HOW POWERFUL YOU ARE.
YOUR INNER LIGHT UNCOVERED
WILL OUTSHINE THE BRIGHTEST STAR.

BELOVED LET ME SHOW YOU
HOW THE STARS WILL BOW IN AWE
WHEN YOU ARISE AGAIN FROM DUST
UNVARNISHED, NUDE AND RAW.

When I am broken,
when I don't know where to go,
when I am lost,
when I feel alone,
when heaviness enters my heart and
pulls me down,
when darkness clouds my vision,
I go in.

Through the portal of my heart,
I enter the realm of unconditional Love
and ask the infinite light of my soul to
embrace the broken human that is me.

And as Love floods my being,
the shouting of my pain subsides.
The fear goes back to sleep.

Once again I am safe in knowing:
I am loved.

BELOVED SOUL, I WISH YOU COULD SEE
WHAT I SEE WHEN I LOOK AT YOU.
YOU ARE SO BEAUTIFUL.
DEEP IN YOUR EYES SHINES THE SOURCE
OF EVERYTHING THAT YOU ARE,
AND IN BRIEF FLASHES YOU ALLOW
YOUR ABUNDANCE OF LIGHT
TO SHINE THROUGH,
BRINGING LOVE TO THE WORLD AROUND YOU
IN A SINGLE ACT OF TRUTHFULLY BEING YOU.
JUST BEING YOU.

I LOVE YOU MORE THAN YOU WILL
EVER UNDERSTAND.
I LOVE EVERYTHING THAT IS YOU.
YOUR PAIN, YOUR DARKNESS, YOUR LIGHT
AND YOUR JOY, EQUALLY AS MUCH.

On the journey through life, every single day, time and time again, you will be offered to take a step closer to the truth of the light that is you. Closer to the Love that you are. You will be offered to let a single layer gently fall from your shoulders, one at a time, until you finally stand naked in all your magnificence, ready to offer to the world everything that is uniquely you.

That is why life is shaking you right now. Shaking off the layers of everything untrue that you have been holding onto. Shaking you until your masks fall off, until the varnish cracks, until you can no longer hide from your own light reminding you of who you are, the one you came to be, the unique expression of God's Love that is you.

God will be with you through it all. Though it may feel like it on a day like this, you are not abandoned. Even in your darkest moments, you are not abandoned. You are so much more important than you can imagine, and with you, you have everything necessary to shield and protect you, to support you and help you, to guide and embrace you. Love itself. Running like an endless river through your entire being.

Everything is Love.

You are Everything.

As God is the ocean and you are a drop
in its vastness of Love and creation,
You can lean back in trust
that through waves and through tides
You are held in the arms of salvation.

As God is the ocean and you are a drop
in the infinite waters of oneness,
You are bigger than biggest
and smaller than small
being part of true Love in abundance.

As God is the ocean and you are a drop
in a unit without separation,
You can never be less
than the fullness of Love
as you've been since the day of creation.

Falling in Love

Every day I fall in love all over again,
recognizing the divine presence
in everything.
Like mirrors spread out by abundant hands,
allowing us to remember the truth of
who we are, as Love is reflected back to us
from the beauty we meet in the glass.

Beloved soul, who do you think you need to be?

Who do you think you need to become, to deserve Love?

How do you think you have to act or feel or think, to enter the kingdom of heaven?

Maybe you have been taught that to enter the embrace of Love, the embrace of God, which is the same, you have to behave in a certain way. You have to be a good girl or a good boy. You have to be kind, act with compassion and always be willing to help those in need. Be sweet, gentle, generous and loving. And yes, we should strive to be all those things. But there is a serious misconception that needs to be cleared: Love works the other way around.

You—yes you, my love—carry within you the door to the kingdom of heaven. The realm of Love. Placed right there in your heart.

And when you have the courage to open that door, when you dare to be vulnerable enough to let go of everything standing in the way of you entering this sacred cathedral within, you will find a world of incredible peace and beauty.

This, my love, is your soul. The part of you that is eternal, the part of you that is divine. The dwelling place of God in you.

Experiencing the nearness of God is like bathing in Love. As if every cell of your body lights up with a profound sense of being filled with the divine presence. Looking out on the world from this place, from this state of connectedness, your perspective changes.

You cannot help but fall in love with the world. Suddenly you recognize the presence of God everywhere. You see the Love that runs through everything. You recognize the light of the divine soul in the eyes of everyone you meet. You feel a deep connection to all living things, and there is nothing or no one you are unable to love, because all is one. All is God.

Now hurting other people as well as yourself is no longer possible. With your heart open, nothing can hold back your compassion in the face of suffering. Every action, every thought, every feeling, every word you speak will spring from Love.

But make no mistake. Love is so much more than sweetness and romance. It is the most powerful force in existence, insisting without compromise on the highest good of all. Feeding you the strength and courage to stand up for your truth. At all times.

Let the echo of true love
paint your world in a different light.
Lift the veil of expectation
for a glimpse of godly might.

See how winds can carry planes and birds
and warmth across the globe.
See how one soul by its actions can ignite
a spark of hope.

See how mighty trees and forests
grow from a tiny potent seed.
See how bodies just like magic
heal themselves from wounds that bleed.

See how kindness heals a heart
that found the world a painful place.
See how life can tell a story
through the wrinkles on your face.

See the stars spread out like mirrors
leading lost souls home at night.
See the miracles around you
as they play out in plain sight.

Fall in love with the world like a child.
See the beauty in everything wild.
Fall in love with the world like a child.
See the beauty in everything wild.

Fall in love with the tastes on your tongue.
Seize the day like the brave and the young.
Fall in love with the sour, bitter, sweet,
giving thanks, blessing life, as you eat.

Fall in love with the smell of rain
like the tingling joy of champagne.
Fall in love with the tang
of your sweat and your tears
as you journey through all of your fears.

Fall in love with the sounds of the sky,
with the singing of birds flying high.
Fall in love with the sound of
the waves on your shore
as they wash off the armor you wore.

Fall in love with yourself as you are,
the loveliest creature by far.
Fall in love with your struggles,
your pain, and your shame.
You will always be loved just the same.

I WILL BE IN THE WIND
WHEN IT'S BLOWING YOUR HAIR.
I WILL BE IN YOUR BREATH,
I WILL BE IN THE AIR.

I WILL BE IN THE SUNBEAMS
CARESSING YOUR SKIN.
I WILL BE IN THE MOONLIGHT
THAT KISSES YOUR CHIN.

I WILL BE IN THE SOUNDS
OF THE RIVERS AND SEAS.
I WILL BE IN THE BUZZING
OF PLEASED HONEYBEES.

I AM PRESENT IN DEATH.
I AM PRESENT IN BIRTH.
I AM HERE EVERY SECOND
OF LIFE ON THIS EARTH.

HOLD EVERYTHING SACRED,
AS ALL THAT YOU SEE
WAS BORN FROM ONE WOMB,
THE SOURCE OF ALL QI.

HOLD EVERYTHING SACRED,
AS ALL THAT YOU MEET
IS TRUE LOVE'S CREATION,
FLAWLESS AND COMPLETE.

HOLD EVERYTHING SACRED,
AS ALL THAT YOU FEEL
IS MY LOVING GUIDANCE
TO HOW YOU CAN HEAL.

HOLD EVERYTHING SACRED,
AS ALL THAT YOU ARE
IS AS PRECIOUS TO ME
AS A BRIGHT MORNING STAR.

As a child, I will venture
through life on a quest,
to discover this magical place
as a guest.

I will touch everything
with the thrill of a first,
let my hands go through
bubbles of soap as they burst.

I will take in the wonders
of smell through my nose,
the rain, the fresh coffee,
the pine and the rose.

Let my lips and my tongue
meet each texture and taste,
nor let any good chance
of a kiss go to waste.

With my eyes wide as skies
I will gaze at the moon,
just wishing that it would
slide down to me soon.

I will run, I will dance,
I will laugh, I will sing,
surrender in awe
of the joy life can bring.

How glorious, glorious,
this life will be
when lived through the senses
of one who can see.

Today I woke up to a marvelous sight
unfolding in front of my eyes.
As if layers of dust had been washed
from my gaze and a new world
appeared from the guise.

I saw glorious cobwebs all covered in
pearls, the treasure of dew
in the morning.
I saw blood–colored leaves in a
breathtaking dance
surrendering as they were falling.

I saw sun rays of gold on a
blue morning sky,
dressing clouds in a fairytale gown.
I saw crystals of frost cover
birches and oaks
majestically worn as their crown.

I saw people in colors
like never before,
all beaming with light from within.
I saw kindness, compassion and
truth in their hearts,
recognized by my soul as my kin.

May this morning forever stay
clear in my mind,
to remind me on days that are harder,
of the spirit around me,
though kept out of sight,
still blessing my soul with its ardor.

Beloved soul, don't let the pain of the moment cast a shadow over that which lies ahead. Your future is full of miracles, moments of great joy, of bliss and meaning. Most likely even this moment of pain will someday make sense.

Your future will also be filled with days like this one. Days that are painful, when things are difficult or there is resistance. I know that for certain because that's how life is. There is no such thing as a painless life, and a great part of the "we" experience is caused by the very idea that it can or should be different.

Life is a playground. A wonderful place full of possibilities in which you have the chance to romp about. Sometimes you may feel butterflies in your stomach when the swings lift you high up in great ecstasy. And sometimes your chair will tilt and you will crash down to the ground with a hard thump that will spread like a pain throughout your entire being.

Everything has its own time and place. It is all part of being a human on this earth and they are all moments that will be replaced by new moments of other qualities. Every high is followed by a low. Every low is followed by a high. It's the nature of life.

Just know that everything is all right and hold yourself in Love until this time of pain has passed. For it will pass. Even the greatest, most unbearable pain will find its place within you and discover new forms so that the two of you can live side by side as the rest of your life unfolds.

A Prayer

Beloved God, in You I pray
that Love will fill my heart today,
that Your presence as a state of mind
will make me true and strong and kind.

Beloved God, today I'll be
what only true Love's eyes can see.
Divinity on earth expressed
awakened from the depth of rest.

Beloved God, I pray that I
may be set free from every lie.
May I be true to what You know
that I am here to share and show.

May I be brave enough to free
the light that shines inside of me.
May I be blessed with eyes that dare
to recognize You everywhere.

May I surrender into You,
be willing to begin anew.
In service, I will bow in awe,
remember what I came here for.

May every action from my hand
bring nurture to this wonderland.
May every step I take today
bless all encounters on my way.

Show me how.

Thank you,

Amen.

Blessed are the ones
with an open heart,
for they shall know God.

Now, all you have to do...

...is close your eyes and listen.

About the Author

Anja Steensig is a Danish spiritual mentor, author and international transformational speaker.

For more than a decade she was one of the best-known television and radio personalities in Denmark. Hosting her own talk show as well as other formats of entertainment, she was voted best female television host during her career.

In 2011 Anja fell into a deep depression that changed her life forever. After six months in painful darkness, she reentered the world completely transformed. Her heart had been blasted opened and she found herself in a state of pure unconditional Love, where she suddenly saw everything from a perspective of Love. She knew that she was no longer in charge of her own life, but a servant of something infinitely bigger. As she surrendered into the loving guidance she received, life took her on a seven-year journey to learn and grow further into the experience and understanding of God expressed as Love.

As she now passes on the wisdom she received, Anja represents what is considered a new Nordic approach to spirituality, in which everything but the direct, pure and simple connection with God is stripped away, uncomplicated and solely focused on how we can bring God's Love more fully into our lives and into the world. This is a simple and honest, non-religious spirituality devoted solely to the service to God.

Anja lives in Denmark with her husband and three children. Learn more about Anja at:

www.anjasteensig.com